WILD ABOUT YOU

Lucky
Chance

By Lyn Ellison

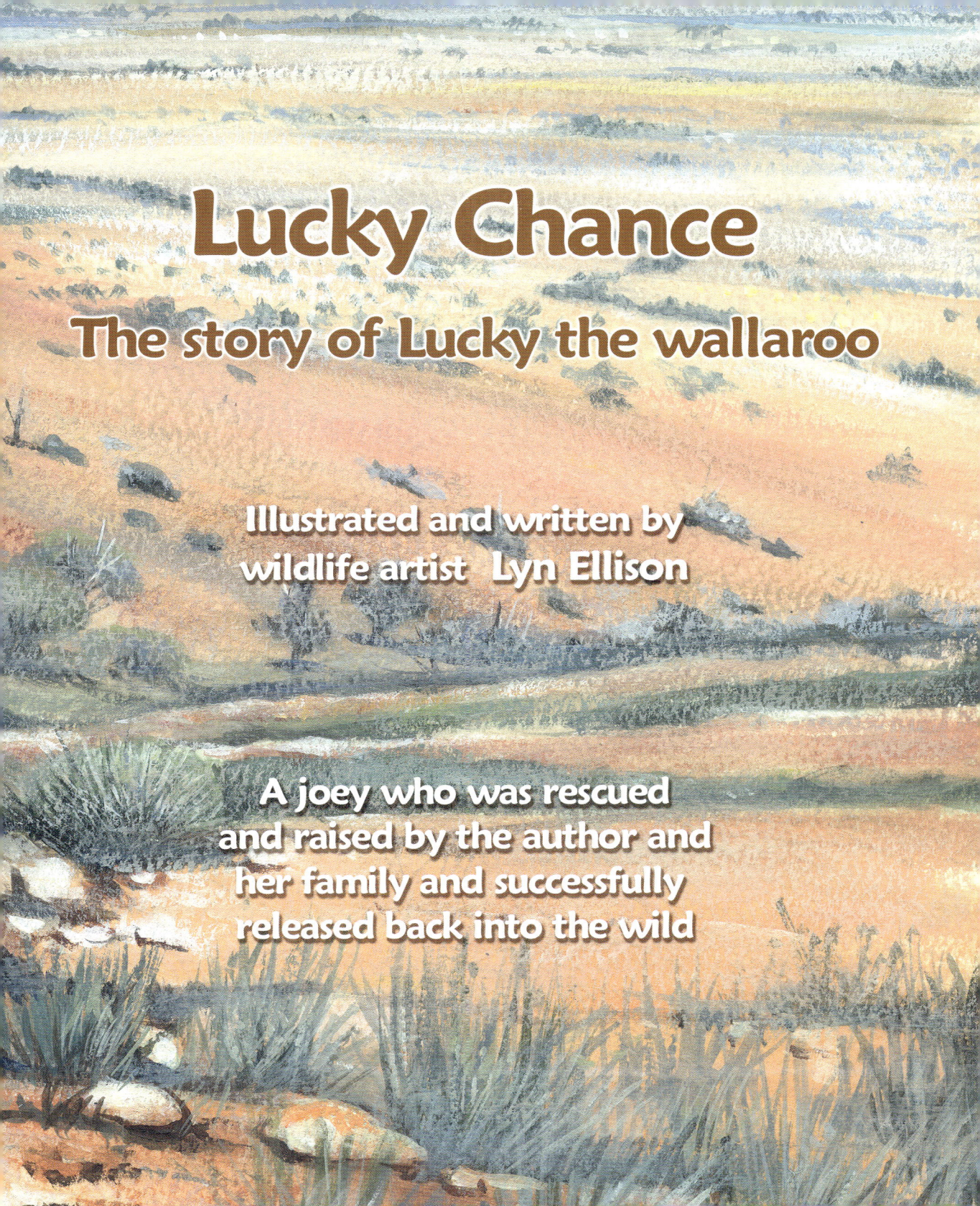

Lucky Chance

The story of Lucky the wallaroo

Illustrated and written by
wildlife artist Lyn Ellison

A joey who was rescued
and raised by the author and
her family and successfully
released back into the wild

This book is dedicated to

Nancy and Orm Ridgway
who are an inspiration to all wildlife carers
and
my husband Don Ellison
who is the ultimate motivator

Other books by Lyn Ellison
'Wild About You - Friends With Feathers'
By Peta Boyce and Lyn Ellison

Published by Magpie Art Prints,
2 Braeside Cres. Maudsland Q'ld 4210 Australia
First published 2000
Illustrations and Text Copyright Lyn Ellison
Printed by Toppan, Hong kong
Design and Layout by Lyn Ellison

National Library of Australia Cataloguing - in Publication Data
Ellison, Lyn, 1943-
Lucky chance.
ISBN 0 9585878 1 7.
1. Wildlife Rescue - Australia. 2.Common wallaroo - Australia.
I. Title. (Series: Wild About You)
599.2220994

Contents

PART ONE

THE WILD STORY

This story begins in the outback where open spaces go on forever and a young wallaroo's day starts at sunset when the air begins to cool. The last rays of the sun touch the spikes of the dusty spinifex and emu bushes that stretch across the plains. The gnarled trunks of the river redgums take on a rosy hue as they wind along the sandy water courses. The air has lost its blinding glare to become soft and hazy with the approach of nightfall. Bird calls fill the air as galahs and corellas settle down for the night and flocks of budgerigars come wheeling in to reach their nesting trees.

A young wallaroo can watch all this from the safety of her mother's pouch high on a rocky ledge. The long, sleepy hours are almost over and she waits impatiently for her mother to move out onto the plain to feed. At some stage in the cool of night the pouch muscles will be released and the joey can tumble out onto the ground to stretch her legs and leap for joy in the moonlight! This is an exciting time for her after being confined to her mother's pouch. It is a time to play and run free.

At 7 months of age her long hind legs are hard to control and she does not always land where she expects. She has sometimes ended up stranded in the middle of a prickly clump of spinifex or hanging by one leg in the branches of a salt bush, but when she gets it right and is bouncing along at full joey speed all those embarrassing moments are quite forgotten. When the joey is out of the pouch her mother watches her carefully and calls her back with a loud clicking sound if she strays too far. The joey knows to return immediately and will dive head first into the pouch leaving her long legs and tail dangling outside. Later, after twisting and wriggling around she will finally poke her head out again.

Just as the mother calls to her joey, a young wallaroo can hiss fiercely when threatened with danger. Once, as the light began to fade, and she was practising her jumps some distance from her mother, she landed close to a bearded dragon. To her dismay the flat looking lizard suddenly became twice its size, puffing itself up and expanding the frill around its neck. Rearing back, it opened its mouth to wheeze horribly and show a set of sharp teeth. The joey, not to be outdone also hissed savagely and with fur standing out all over looked larger and nastier too. It was hard to tell who looked the fiercest as they stood there facing each other, neither daring to look away. They both found it hard to keep up the pretence for long, each one waiting for the other to make a move. The stand off ended in an anticlimax with both parties shrinking back to size and darting away in opposite directions.

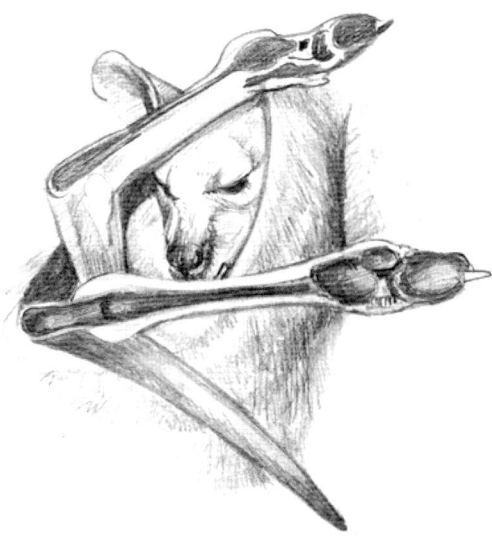

Although a mother wallaroo can move with speed across the plains, her joey can be a very heavy load. Her pouch bulges like a sports bag crammed with gear and when she browses her hind legs are splayed out awkwardly, short arms supporting her as she leans forward. In this position the joey's head is quite close to the ground and what her mother eats can be sampled by the youngster too. It is also possible for the joey to reach out and grasp twigs and stalks of grass or pull branches of low shrubs close enough to study. In this way she learns to recognise the plants and grasses her mother browses on and by the time she is fully weaned she will know exactly what to eat.

As she hangs out of the pouch an intriguing world can be studied beneath her nose and her curiosity is constantly aroused. As the sun goes down, she watches insects busily tracking across the sandy ground, digging holes and weaving webs. Small lizards dart here and there and tiny black ants carry heavy loads back to their nests. She watches the ants with particular interest as they race back and forth, wondering if they are edible. The painful sneezing frenzy that follows her close investigation, convinces her that ants are definitely not on the menu! Such a setback does not seem to dampen her interest and she is soon studying the insect world again.

A time will come later when this young wallaroo will be tipped out of the pouch for the last time. She will try to force her way back in but her mother will tighten her muscles and keep the pouch closed. This is a sad time for the joey because all she has known is the warmth and security of her mother's pouch. Unknown to the young wallaroo, a new life is stirring in her mother and another hairless, bean-size wallaroo is waiting to be born and make the long climb through the fur to the pouch. Here it will attach itself to its own teat and remain there until it in turn grows too big.

Her mother is so specialized she can produce a different kind of milk for each of her offspring. One milk is suited to the robust life of a joey and another for the needs of a fragile new baby.

The young wallaroo will stay close to her mother for the next few months and though she will be allowed to suckle, her feet will be firmly on the ground. Her eating habits will change until she is eating mainly native grasses and plants and she will forage further and further away from the security of her mother until she finds herself alone. The long dependency on her mother will then be over and she will be equipped to survive in the sparse country that stretches far and wide around her. She will be familiar with the wide area that represents her mother's territory and will know where water can be found in the driest times and the best places to find food throughout the year.

The opportunity to follow her mother and learn to survive did not arise for the wallaroo in this story. Instead something catastrophic happened to change her life. On one particular night that started off like many others, the joey and her mother moved out across the plains to feed. The rosy light of evening had faded as the moon climbed into the sky and the pair found themselves on the edge of a sandy watercourse. River redgums loomed above their heads and in a hollow, water glimmered. Listening for unfamiliar sounds they made their way towards the waterhole where many other animals had come to drink. A red kangaroo stood rubbing the water from its whiskers while on the far bank a thirsty echidna tested the air with its nose.

The joey looked longingly at the hills of sand rising from the water's edge. What a place to get out of the pouch and play! But the air hung strangely still, the shadows beneath the trees appeared secretive and her mother did not relax. Instead she turned her ears and lifted her nose. Something was wrong tonight! The joey watched with frightened eyes no longer eager to tumble out. A curlew called and made her mother cough with fear. In that instant a blur of yellow fur flashed across the sand. Reacting immediately her mother took a huge leap and the pair took off towards the far bank and the deeper shadows. But the going was slow on the sandy bank and the dingo had the advantage of surprise. They needed to gain some speed, with the dingo close behind, so they left the sand and zigzagged through the trees the mother wallaroo using all her skills to keep the pair alive. Her mother had been chased before and knew she would eventually have to head for open ground.

To widen the gap between them she made a supreme effort to lengthen her strides, pumping extra power through her strong legs. Now she was out on the open plain and if she did not out run the dingo there would be nowhere to hide. Even though her mother was heavily burdened the dingo began to drop behind a little. Instinct told the joey that they were in grave danger, that here was

an enemy of great stamina and strength and her mother would need all her skills to survive tonight. Sometimes a wallaroo will throw her joey out of the pouch to lighten her load and lead the dingo off in another direction. In this case the mother kept to her course and maintained her speed. The joey was jolted and bumped in the wild race but the distance was widening between them and the predator. Finally the dingo was left far behind standing exhausted and alone in the middle of the plain.

Now the youngster expected her mother to slow down but instead she kept on going. Bruised and battered the joey now saw that the countryside they raced through was unfamiliar. When would her mother stop? Where was she going? The joey did not know that stress had taken hold of her mother and that her survival skills were in tatters. When the dazzling lights ahead went unnoticed and she kept on, unconscious of any danger, the little wallaroo knew something terrible was about to happen. The lights and the fearful noise were on top of them before her mother tried to change her course. By then it was too late and in a flash the pair was tossed into the air as the world exploded around them. The mother wallaroo would not go back to her rocky ledge to see another day.

When the first rays of the sun touched her mother, crushed on the road, the joey lay alive, but cold and frightened in a pouch that no longer felt secure. There was no answering movement, no reassuring warmth to fill the pouch. What had happened to her mother? .

Clutching the edge of the pouch she gazed at the line of red gums stretching across the plains and watched the last of the birds take off into the sky. Although she could climb out of the pouch and leap away to find a place to hide, this idea was worse than staying on the road. Her mother had never been out of sight and instinct told her to stay put. Already something had roared by within inches of her feet and she had felt such terror that she could hardly breathe.

When footsteps sounded on the road close by, the frightened joey was alert again, survival instincts giving her new strength. A strange and terrifying animal bent down to stare at her with anxious eyes. The frightened youngster took her deepest breath and gave her loudest hiss! A savage hiss, one which would have certainly made her mother proud! The affect was startling and caused the ugly creature to jump back and gasp in fear, just as the lizard had done some time before when life had felt so safe with her mother standing near.

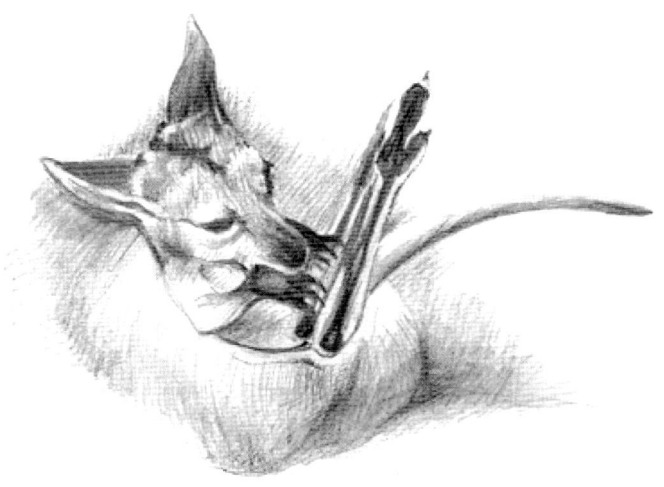

PART TWO

THE FOSTER STORY

What a morning it was! My husband Don and I were in high spirits as we travelled home on yet another outback road. This one stretched out across a wide, dry plain of spinifex and dusty scrub. Birds rose from their roost trees along a river bed to fill the morning with their calls. All along the road places caught our eye, worthy of a stop, and over the next hill maybe there was something else to take our breath away! The beauty of the morning seemed to be for us alone. Then we saw the slaughter on the road.

At first we hardly noticed a kangaroo or two lying dead beside the road but as we travelled further on the number increased. To our horror we saw kangaroos strewn everywhere, in places three or four together in a heap. As very little traffic passed this way it looked as though a road train had ploughed through here last night, never changing from its course, never even slowing for the poor unwary animals.

Our mood was cheerless as we drove along, slowing here and there to go around the dead. As we came across another body in the middle of the road Don leaned across to have a better look.

'Looks like something moved in that one's pouch! Surely something's still alive out there!' Don said.

After pulling off the road with the caravan in tow, I hurried back towards the bodies, full of hope. Maybe something had survived the night. And so it had! Lying there amongst the broken bones and wasted lives was a joey, perfect and untouched and it seemed as though something had kept her safe for us to find.

As I bent down to touch the little animal, it drew itself together, took a

deep breath and let out a fierce hiss. I yelled out in fright and fell over backwards as I jumped away.

'You should have seen your face! Oh dear, what a sight! You would have thought it was a snake and not a joey in the pouch!' laughed Don as he caught up with me. I felt so foolish being scared of such a small defenceless creature. When I recovered, I pulled the dead mother off the road, wondering how long it would have been before another car had come along and crushed them both. The body was not a heavy weight to shift and I wondered what kind of kangaroo or wallaby she was with her lovely sandy coat and black tipped tail. I had to steel myself to pull the joey from the pouch as it clung tightly to its mother's fur. The last connection with the mother would now be broken, the close bond gone, and everything that seemed secure and safe was lost. The poor little joey! It looked so frightened and helpless. With a rush of tenderness I wrapped it in a towel and held it tightly in my arms. A new bond was about to be formed, on my part at least!

Back in the caravan we had a close look at the little joey. There was no sign of injury, its manner seemed quite bright and there was no doubt she was a female with her perfect little pouch. Her eyes, ears and hind legs all looked much too big for the rest of her but every detail was perfect. The black skin on her nose and the bottom of her feet and hands looked freshly polished and her fur was soft and clean. Her little face was shaded from dark grey to creamy white. The rest of her fur was a mixture of soft greys and sandy pinks with fine white fur on her chest and belly. She was a beautiful creature and we wondered how old she was as she looked quite small. We were captivated when she gazed at us with her enormous black eyes. Our beautiful morning was restored again.

'What do we do now? We haven't got a clue how to feed her and we don't know a thing about raising a baby kangaroo!'

The weight of responsibility hit me. I needed to *do something*. We mixed low fat milk with boiled water and gave it to her on a teaspoon. She took this thirstily as though it was the normal way to drink. I turned my large quilted toilet bag into a 'pouch' and lined it with a towel. (My 'essentials' were now lost in chaos at the bottom of a plastic shopping bag.) I held her in my arms and tried to reassure her and I worried a lot.

Wise after the event, we now know we should have put her in a much deeper bag which covered her head and left her quietly on her own to adjust to the traumatic experience. Her mother's milk was very low in lactose and cows milk is very high so her first feed could have been a disaster too! She was probably too quiet as well, for that first hiss was the only sound she made.

When we finally drove on she gazed at us quietly over the top of the bag, arms crossed demurely on her chest. From my lap she watched our faces and studied the inside of the 4WD with serious black eyes. I wondered what she thought of us and the strange situation she was in. To be dragged out of her mother's pouch and dumped into the arms of a totally strange creature must have been terrifying and yet she gazed at us with what looked like trust.

'I've just had great idea, why don't we call Jan?' I said. 'Didn't she raise a baby kangaroo?' I had been worrying about feeding the joey and when we came into range with our mobile phone, we made a frantic call. Jan soothed our fears, told us what sort of milk to buy (Digestalac) and how much to give her.

'Oh, I am excited for you! It will be a unique experience if you decide to raise her. Our 'Mali' was such a joy. Of course your little joey will need at least 5 bottle feeds a day and you will have to get up and feed her in the middle of the night.' were her parting words.

Why is it always Sunday when there is an emergency? When we finally reached the next town the shops seemed to be closed and very few people were about. How were we going to find the things we needed for her?

'She'll die if we don't find a chemist!' I wailed. 'What are we going to do?'

I am sure the man who raced over to give us directions must have thought we had a real baby! The chemist we were directed to had the right milk and the right bottles and though the bottles looked more like those for feeding dolls than thirsty kangaroos, they did the trick. In no time at all she was drinking milk from a bottle as though she had always done it this way and her foster mother was calm again.

It was a long trip home. The constant movement of the car, the strangeness of the two ugly creatures taking care of her and the frightening sounds and smells, must have been very hard on her. Every so often she would shake violently which did not look good and I hoped this would stop when we finally got home. When we pulled up for a break and I put her on the grass to stretch her legs she would sniff around timidly but as soon as I moved away she would hop after me, desperately trying to get back into her pouch. There was no chance of losing her!

We tried sleeping with her at night to keep her warm but she would fidget and eventually fall out of the pouch and down the gap between the bed and the wall. It was no easy job untangling a long legged joey from such a narrow space, and in the dark! Finally we wedged her between pillows on the lounge and often by morning she would be out of the pouch, and bumping round on the floor looking for breakfast.

'Thank goodness we are in a caravan! Just imagine trying to hide her in a motel room every night. How would we explain all the bumps and crashes the next morning?' I said.

'I think that would have been the least of our worries' Don said dryly.

Choosing names for our little charge took up some of the time driving home. There was no doubt she was 'lucky'. The road was very lonely where we found her and she would have stayed in the pouch until she died. If a car had gone by it probably would have driven right over her. 'Lucky' seemed quite suitable in the circumstances and it stuck.

The drive home also gave me plenty of time to think and worry. I made mountains out of molehills and nearly drove Don mad.

'How on earth can we combine three dogs and a kangaroo? What a welcoming committee the dogs will be!' I moaned. 'Sandy will want to kill Lucky' (Sandy was part dingo).

'Oh it will never work! How can we raise a kangaroo without fences?'

Don stayed calm as usual and worked out most of my problems. By the time we arrived home I was smiling optimistically and ready to raise a joey under any circumstances.

We left Lucky in the caravan, sitting in the middle of our double bed looking about brightly and told our daughter to go and see what we had brought back. She read something in our faces and I am sure she was resigned to finding some poor injured bird or animal more dead than alive. Instead she found a perfect little joey and was won over immediately.

Life settled down remarkably quickly. After the first shock of having to share their home with a kangaroo, the dogs resigned themselves to the new order. Sandy gave her menacing stares. Tawny, my shadow, began sleeping on our bed at night. Patches, the quiet one, kept her distance and Bubby our overweight cat seemed glad to have another animal smaller than herself. Little did she know what was in store!

Lucky slept in our bedroom to begin with, safe inside a baby's play pen. Or so I thought! The first morning she climbed out of her pouch, squeezed through the slats and stood beside the bed clicking loudly for breakfast. Tawny the doberman, with eyes wide open in disbelief, watched all this from the middle of our bed convinced that her last stronghold was about to be invaded! And so the bedroom phase was very short and the lounge room became Lucky's domain.

'*A kangaroo in my lounge room*' could have been the title of this book! For the next 12 months 'princess' Lucky lived in comfort here, reclining on soft cushions on the lounge while keeping a close eye on her subjects. A screen door was put in place to keep the dogs out and some furniture moved when she found she could jump onto our drinks bar and come visiting on our side of the barricade. A 'cat door' was also installed later so she could go outside into her 'yard' whenever she liked, (which was not very often).

'What sort of kangaroo is she?' I asked myself. Looking through my collection of Australian wildlife books I could not find a likeness to Lucky in any of the pictures, however hard I tried.

'She must be a red kangaroo, nothing else looks remotely like her!' I decided. When I phoned a local wildlife rescue group to ask their advice, I told them she was a red kangaroo. Of course I was wrong!

'She's not big and gangly enough for a red kangaroo,' said the experienced macropod carer I was put in touch with. 'She's a wallaroo joey! We don't get many of these into care. What a little beauty!'

Wallaroos are known to be feisty and independent and live more solitary lives than other types of kangaroo. Distinguishing features include a black hairless area around the nostrils, a thickset body, shaggy fur and big feet!. No wonder Lucky was such a 'miss'! Right from the start she was very much her own animal. She would lift her nose and look at me with an amused and knowing manner as if to say *'I've done all this before you know!'* Although she came to depend on me for love and companionship, deep within her eyes I could see she kept a lot of wild secrets just for herself.

I was shown how to calculate Lucky's age. By weighing her and measuring her feet and tail I judged her to be seven months old. At 1.75 kilos she still

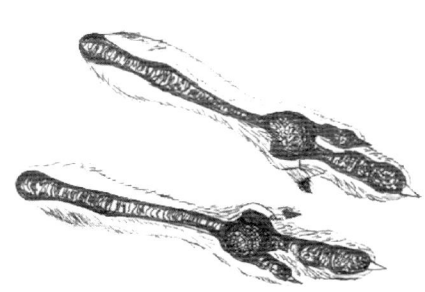

had a long way to go before I would release her into the wild as an eighteen month old teenager weighing 11 kilos. For the next twelve months I would weigh and measure Lucky frequently as she grew and compare this with records of other wallaroos raised by carers, to be sure she was developing and putting on weight properly.

'Does Lucky really need that many pouches?' Don laughed.

Within a few weeks I had a large collection of pouches for Lucky, all of them essential! There were 'apron pouches' designed to wear while doing my housework. These were based on a mother kangaroo with the pouch hanging from my waist and though I drew the line at actually hopping, Lucky enjoyed being mobile and closely watched everything I did. That Christmas I even cooked the festive meal with Lucky in my pouch! Studying home science may not have been essential training for a young wallaroo, but it kept her amused. I loved to answer the door in my pouch outfit just to see the amazement on people's faces!

There were canvas backpacks designed for outdoor walks when the dogs and I took our daily exercise. We would walk down to the river and

follow the bank along, stopping at favourite places to throw sticks and watch for platypus and birds. Of course Lucky joined the gang and as soon as I lifted her into her backpack the dogs would bark madly. Off we would all troop, dogs leaping around me, Lucky hanging out behind and me stomping along in my 'snake' boots. It must have been a funny sight! The walk included barbed wire fences and steep banks so I pinned the bag securely with giant safety pins, just in case! Lucky continued to join us on these walks until she was 9 kilos in weight and too heavy to carry any more. Once we met an American girl working on the next property. She did not seem shocked, though I wondered what she told the folks back home!

'This little joey has such bright eyes' she exclaimed, 'all the kangaroos I have seen in captivity have vacant eyes.' It was a comment I have not forgotten.

A 'car pouch' was designed so I could take her with me to visit my parents. She seemed to enjoy the drive and the opportunity to explore another house but the main reason was to prepare her for future journeys. In an emergency, a trip to the local 'vet' would then not be such a trauma and always in the back of my mind was that final trip I would have to make to set her free. Lucky loved having 'afternoon tea' with my parents and she became very fond of weak black tea but she eventually grew too big to go visiting.

The pouches already described were the 'mobile' ones! The 'super-special' pouch she used in our lounge room was designed by the wildlife carers group. This featured a hessian bag with one side made into a pouch, stretched over an inverted U shaped frame, with feet to stop it from toppling over. The pouch hung just off the floor so an active joey could dive in or out safely. A creature of comfort like Lucky could loll here, half asleep, with her legs sticking up in the air and her arms trailing over the side. She could reach tempting titbits like grapes and pecans or a pile of grass without much effort! Of course the original design was adapted so the unglamorous hessian was hidden with soft inner linings and colourful blankets.

'Lucky is having another 'grass party!' we would often say.

There she would be, sitting up brightly in her 'super pouch', in party mood, with a plate of grass resting on top of a large dictionary in front of her. At first she would try to grasp the stalks and poke them into her mouth but come party time she would be tossing grass around all over the room or stuffing it in her pouch.

I am not an early riser but while Lucky was with us I got up at 6 a.m. without any qualms, knowing that she would be awake at dawn and watching out for me from then on.

Early morning was our special time together when everyone else was still in bed and the dogs were shut outside. When she was older I spent this time out in her 'paddock' trying to convince her that the outdoors was a great place for a wallaroo to be, but in the early months the house was her domain. Her bottle of milk was always first priority and if she was out waiting by the barricade, there would be a frantic effort to dive back into the pouch I held out for her. She would then wriggle around until her head poked out and with a sigh of contentment lie back on my lap, hold the bottle in her paws and gaze into my face. We both enjoyed this time when the house was quiet and peaceful and I could allow my maternal instincts full play!

As we had the whole house to ourselves when she had finished her feed, the barricades would come down, the outside doors were safely closed and Lucky could go exploring! While I cleaned up the lounge room after the night's activities, she would play a game with a box of tissues. This involved pulling as many tissues out of the box as she could and tossing them all over the place. The tissues then got the flattening treatment as she jumped on each one until it was flattened into submission. When she was satisfied with this she would follow me through the house to the laundry and play around there while I did the washing. On the way to the laundry there was always plenty to check out so she often arrived well after me.

Bubby the cat was usually dawdling towards her food dish at this stage of the morning so if Lucky sped up she could get there before the cat and have first look. Bubby was much bigger than Lucky in the early months (this was a very overweight cat!) and Lucky would have to back off fast when the cat eventually arrived or risk having her nose scratched. Later, when Lucky out grew Bubby, she got her own back and played some terrible tricks on her. I think they actually liked each other, sharing a bond as the two small ones in the family.

Further along her route she would pause to listen at the door to the master bedroom. She loved to go in here and would try and judge what stage things were at, whether Tawny had been kicked off the bed and put outside or was still being sooked by her master. If I forgot to close the door to my daughter's room as I went past, Lucky would be in there like a shot and after a close inspection of all the clothes on the floor, would jump straight onto the bed. Here she would contemplate the lump under the covers for some time before jumping on it and trying to flatten it out with her hind feet, just like the tissues! Wails and angry noises would come from under the sheets.

'Mum! Get your wallaroo off me! Can't you control your animal! How come you never remember to shut the door? Aaww! She hurts you know!' Lucky would then move on to more interesting places pleased with the reaction she had received from the 'lump'. Merryon would then get up and slam the door shut!

Eventually she would notice my absence and thunder down the hall in a panic, coming to a halt at the laundry door. Relieved to see me, she would hover there for a few minutes and then drift off towards Don's office further down the hall. The laundry held no real interest once she had climbed under the ironing board a few times but the office was prime exploring country. This was not an orderly room! It had stacks of correspondence in trays, piles of magazines and books and boxes of seeds and horticultural samples. It was heaven to a curious young wallaroo. If I stuck my head through the door I might see Lucky with her head and shoulders buried in the waste paper bin, the contents strewn all over the floor while she checked out the depths for hidden treasures. Lots of Don's letters had corners sucked or chewed off but her crumpling efforts were her most 'creative'. She would take a piece of paper (preferably an important letter and not a bill) and crumple it between her paws or press it possessively against her chest for minutes at a time. The same intensive treatment was also given to a stiff piece of packaging tape which she would try to collect up in a ball against her chest only to have it spring out of control again. I remembered reading about young eastern grey kangaroos playing with dry cakes of cow dung in the same manner and wondered what this kind of play related to in the development of a joey. Lucky never tired of exploring this room and it showed just how inquisitive a joey could be.

'Come on Lucky. You've made enough mess in there!' I would call on my way back to the kitchen. This usually fell on deaf ears until she had finished investigating or crushing the particular item on which she was focused.

Again she would notice I was gone and come racing back, rounding the hall corner on 'a wing and a prayer' and skidding over the family room tiles out of control. Bubby was bravely stretched out on the floor by now and Lucky would clear her in a leap before pulling up beside me out of breath. Before long she would be off exploring again.

"Lucky, don't be such a sticky beak! Get out of the dishwasher! I'm sure last night's dinner tastes good but stop licking the plates!'

The dishwasher was fun because she could stand on the door when it was open. This allowed her easy access to a range of forbidden utensils that were covered in interesting tastes and smells. She seemed to think tomato sauce and custard quite suitable for a wallaroo's diet. It was just as good if the dishwasher was empty as she could peer right inside and see another rather distorted wallaroo reflected in the stainless steel!

Our kitchen has a walk-in pantry and as Don loves to shop the shelves are always groaning with food. The more mundane things like dog biscuits and potatoes are stacked on the floor and she could look in all the bags, testing and tasting. Often she would just stand there gazing up at the shelves.

Perhaps she was looking for her pecan nuts or wondering how one family could eat so much!

As soon as she heard the refrigerator door open she would race over and push in front of me to check the crisper for sticks of celery or spring onions that were sticking out. These were right at her level and by the time I was ready to close the door the protruding vegetables were all neatly trimmed off.

By now the house was starting to wake up and it would be time for Lucky to go back behind her barricade or into the safety of my apron pouch. Usually she retired to the lounge room to take a nap, quite satisfied with her morning activities.

Later in the morning I usually went to my 'studio' to paint. I shared this room with the three dogs who liked to keep me company, ranged around my easel in their bean bags. The room always smelt of wet dogs and the concrete floor was usually covered in dog hair. This annoyed me as I often found dog hairs sticking to my paintings but for some reason I had never thought of painting elsewhere. With the arrival of Lucky I packed up and moved to a corner of the lounge room to keep her company and have stayed there ever since! No more dog hairs or doggy smells, just a wallaroo in a pouch on the back of my chair and three jealous dogs eyeballing me through the barricade!

In the early days Lucky did a lot of sleeping, only getting out of the pouch occasionally if she thought her bottle was late and then diving head first back into the pouch as soon as I appeared. As she grew, the time spent out of the pouch increased and if I was in the room she would potter around, playing with her various 'toys.' An old tennis ball of Tawny's was a favourite. She would pick this up and hold it in her arms until it eventually slipped through and rolled away, then she would chase it and start all over again. A similar game was played with a rubber toy that squeaked and once it was dropped she loved to jump on it to make a noise. She also tried this with a teddy bear but however hard she stomped on the bear it would never squeak. Her disappointment was obvious and may have been the reason for later games with the cat!

Lucky's foster mother was the best toy of all and two or three times a day I would have to 'play fight' with her. This involved kneeling down and letting her hold my hands between her paws. Then, standing at full height, balancing on the tips of her toes and tail she would scrabble her paws up and down my arms and whack my hands, like a sparing partner. It sounds nasty, and wallaroos do have long claws, but I received very few scratches. She would get very excited and do a circuit of the lounge room at full speed before bounding in for another bout. Often she ambushed me by changing direction and making a surprise attack from another side. I wondered if she had played like this with her wild mother and what it all signified. We played this game throughout her time with us and as she grew older she liked to throw in a kick or two for good measure! She managed this by balancing on her tail and lifting her back legs off the ground. It was done so fast you would have missed it if you blinked. I thought I would eventually get kicked in the stomach or have my knee caps rearranged but by good luck or good management she never connected. Lucky played a less endearing game in the first few months. She loved to bite! If you look inside a macropod's mouth you will see a solid 'V' representing the upper molars and a chisel shape representing the lower ones. Great for chopping off tough grass and shrubs but excruciating if applied to the back of the arm or leg! Poor Merryon our daughter received more of this tenderizing treatment than I did. Time spent with Lucky often ended with an angry cry.

'That's it! I'm never going near your wallaroo again! Look at the bruise!'

Fortunately she outgrew this painful habit and Merryon forgave her.

A couple of months after Lucky arrived we realized that she could not spend all her time in the house. To make the transition back to the wild she needed an outside enclosure where she could experience all kinds of weather and learn to find food for herself. This was easier said than done! The enclosure was not so hard to build, the difficult part was convincing Lucky to use it! She seemed quite fearful of being outside on her own and it always appeared to be too windy, too wet or too dark after the safe atmosphere of the lounge room.

We were advised to build her fences at least two metres high and as she needed a large area to exercise in, this ended up being costly. Using the wall of the house as one side of the enclosure helped slightly but after I had enlarged the area three times all my helpers went on strike, feeling they had relocated enough star pickets and chain wire fencing!

'The yard looks big enough for a herd of elephants! How big is Lucky supposed to grow anyway?' laughed Don.

We built the enclosure beside the house so that we could see her from both the lounge room and the kitchen but giving her access from the lounge room to the yard was a hard problem to solve. Watching the cat

and dogs use their 'cat door' gave me an idea. 'Do you think Lucky would use a cat door? Could a wallaroo work out how to use such a thing?' I wondered.

Most wildlife carers seem to raise their joeys in a laundry that has convenient access to the back yard but somehow that did not happen at our house. Then again, 'a wallaroo in my laundry' does not have quite the same ring to it!

A 'roo door' was certainly worth a try, so we had one built into the large window in the lounge room. Lucky surprised us. She understood what the door was for, from the minute I called to her on the other side. *No big deal, all the other animals in the house had their own designer door so why not me!* The cat had taken six months learn how to use hers!

With that problem solved we now had to convince her that it was fun to stay outside. To start with she would give the yard one frightened look, dash back in through her 'roo door' and do a nose dive into her pouch.

The only way I could keep her outside was to take her and the 'super pouch', frame and all, and set it up under the trees. From here she was happy to study her new surroundings, eat a few delicacies within reach but *never* set foot outside the pouch.

'I hope I haven't gone to all this trouble and expense for nothing Lucky' I complained.

I repeatedly tipped her out of her pouch but after a couple of anxious moments she would dive back in. We all despaired. Each of us spent time with her outside, reading books, having morning tea, sketching for paintings, but she still remained anchored to her pouch.

Gradually her confidence grew until she felt safe enough to spend short periods alone in her yard. I continued to get up early to give her the first

bottle of milk for the day but instead of messing around in the house we spent the time pottering around her enclosure, studying everything with great interest. This early morning stroll with Lucky was a joy for both of us and one of my special memories.

The yard consisted of a large area of grass and shady trees with a deep cover of leaf mould underneath. We knew wallaroos liked rocky outcrops but getting a truck load of rocks was a bit much, so we settled for a big tree trunk which she could jump over or stand on. When Lucky and I did the 'rounds' in the morning I found she was intensely interested in everything around her, as long as she had company. I could imagine her travelling alongside her mother, taking in every detail of her surroundings and I felt sad that I could only offer her such a restricted area.

Eventually she began to eat things that grew outside and would chew the bark off the trees, pull low branches down and taste the leaves and hold sticks and wood chips from the garden between her paws and grind them up with her strong teeth. Her favourite 'wild' food was the long grass that grew along the fence and the flowers that hung down like soft pink tassels from the powder puff bushes. Her best loved outdoor toy was a piece of weathered bone which she chewed or carried round in her paws.

When it was time for me to go inside and leave her, I would hear the 'roo door' bang soon after and Lucky would be back inside as well! I vowed I would shut her out, but I could never find the heart, knowing the lounge room was her safe haven. At night I did narrow her lounge room 'refuge' down to a small area just inside the 'roo door.' I hoped this would encourage her to spend most of her time outside like wallaroos would do in the wild. Unfortunately she was even more scared of her yard at night and spent long hours looking out the window in a lonely vigil, watching for the things that 'went bump in the night'.

There was a resident brush tailed possum who made nasty grunting noises in the trees, a boobook owl that 'mopoked' sadly and visiting fruit bats that flapped eerily across the yard and occasionally called out like someone being strangled. It was enough to make any young joey's blood curdle!

Not long after the enclosure was built, a violent electrical storm struck in the middle of the night. Being inexperienced in joey- raising I had no idea what an impact this would have on her. The thunder was deafening as we lay awake in bed and the lightening lit up our bedroom as it streaked across the sky. Soon the rain was pouring down, adding to the noise.

'I wonder how Lucky is handling this? I suppose she would be used to storms.' I said casually.

When I checked the lounge room it was empty and there was no sign of her in the yard when I shone a torch out there.

'Lucky's missing!' I shouted and got everyone out of bed in a flash.

In no time I was outside in the pouring rain in my night gown and bare feet sloshing around her enclosure. At first I could see no sign of her and imagined the small joey had jumped the two metre fence! It is hard to be rational in the middle of the night with rain running down your neck!

I eventually found her in the far corner of the yard, right up against the fence, soaking wet and shivering. I am sure if the fence had not been there she would have gone for miles. It was a miserable little Lucky that we brought back inside and wrapped in a towel. We all fussed over her and I gave her a bottle and nursed her until she calmed down and seemed herself again.

From all appearances Lucky seemed unaffected by the drama of the night before. I made a mental note to be there for her next time we had a storm and then forgot about the incident. Three days later Lucky was a very sick joey. At first she had a mild case of diarrhoea but later when this got worse, I panicked and called my macropod expert.

'It could be an internal parasite or it could be 'coccidiosis'. Keep your fingers crossed that it's not the latter. If it is, you have one sick little joey on your hands and you will need to act quickly. A joey can go down hill very fast, so get a sample of her faeces in to the local 'vet' for testing immediately. Has anything unusual happened to her lately?' she finally asked.

It struck me straight away, of course, it was the thunder storm!

'She was frightened by the thunder storm the other night. Could that have caused the trouble?' I asked, shaken myself, by this stage.

'That's it! Kangaroos and wallabies are the most easily stressed animals I know! Stress can kill a kangaroo faster than anything. Take Lucky to the 'vet' right away and tell them to give her a Vitamin E shot. That will help with the stress. As soon as you hear the results of the test, call me,' she said.

I had a sinking feeling as I put down the phone. *A joey can go down hill very fast'*, kept ringing in my ears as I took Lucky to see the local 'vet'. Here they assured me the tests would be done quickly and a limp little Lucky hardly noticed her injection.

Later when I had been given the results of the tests and told my wildlife coordinator the bad news, she was reassuring and full of practical advice. 'Well at least we've caught the coccidiosis early and she's had the Vitamin E to lower her stress. What you do now is treat her with Baycox.'

It was touch and go with Lucky for some time but gradually she regained her vitality as her digestive system settled down again. Throughout the crisis I had been as distressed as a mother with a sick child and I realized how close I had grown to this cheeky little wallaroo. Looking back I can see how fortunate I was to have such sound advice and Lucky's feisty nature to pull her through.

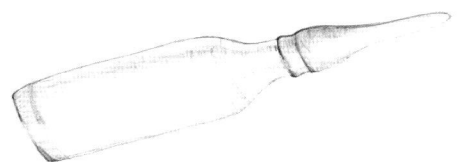

Wallaroos are supposed to be able to survive without water in the wild when conditions are harsh and dry. No one told Lucky this and for a wallaroo she could certainly drink! When she first came into our care I gave her five bottle feeds of milk a day. This was appropriate for her age and size and she loved every minute of the feeds, drinking her milk with gusto. I was advised to give her a special formula for macropods, called Biolac, and this suited her well. She also needed specially designed teats to fit her mouth and simulate her mother's nipple. While she was still confined to her pouch I used to put a bowl of water close by, thinking she would need it in the summer heat. Lucky thought the water was a plaything and spent all day nearly falling out of her pouch, lapping the water and splashing it with her paws. If I sat beside her with my cup of black tea she would always poke her nose into my cup and finish it off with loud slurps! All this extra fluid caused a few 'accidents' and we had some very soggy pouches, so the water bowl had to go. When my friend, Barbara, a potter, heard about Lucky's tea drinking habits she made her a Japanese-style tea bowl. This became her favourite utensil and from then on she always started her day with a cup of warm black tea!

As Lucky progressed and spent more time out of the pouch, she finally became interested in dry food. She loved the soft, long grass that grew down near the river and I would cut her an armful every morning to put with the assortment of foods she had for breakfast. Muesli, rolled oats and puffed corn were all part of the menu, as well as slices of apple, sweet potato and carrot. Grapes and pecan nuts were by far her favourites, so these had to be rationed. She often waited hopefully at the barricade for one of these delicacies to materialize and of course it often did, as we indulged her. If I had pecans tucked away in any of my pockets she always found them quickly and foraged away with her nose until she had emptied the contents.

'Look what Lucky's done to one of your good art books! How can you let her chew your books?' Merryon would say when she saw another of my books with the cover 'rearranged'.

Lucky was definitely partial to paper and included it in her diet at every opportunity. It did not seem to harm her and I suppose in the wild she would have chewed on bark and sticks. As all our books were kept in the lounge room, we eventually had to partition this area off, so that Lucky could not nibble on them when she was hungry. With these out of reach she chewed on phone books instead. These were used to block up gaps in her barricade and we would laugh to see her dozing, with her head resting on a telephone book as though she had fallen asleep half way through eating all the 'Ms'.

My art paper must have been tasty too as I have often had to retrieve half finished drawings from her clutches. I can still picture her standing on the

coffee table holding a full sized, cut out drawing of a magpie in her paws, while she proceeded to eat its beak off. I had probably spent a couple of hours drawing up the magpie and I should have been angry. Instead I just laughed at the sight, such was her effect on me!

Lucky had a definite pattern to her life once she was out of the pouch. For much of the day she lazed around, either lying stretched out on the carpet or draped across a large soft footstool. In between dozes she might languidly pick at her food or go for a stroll around her enclosure, but nothing strenuous. Towards late afternoon she became more active and demanded a sparring partner for her arm wrestling or a spectator for her speed runs around the yard. Here she would do a few warm up laps to stretch her long back legs before gathering speed, jumping the log, avoiding the trees and doing circles around whoever was watching. Sometimes she lost it on the turns and slipped sideways, coming to an undignified stop against the fence. She put so much energy into this it was hard to believe she was the same animal who had been lazing around a few hours before.

Her nights were spent going for short excursions out into the dark and then rushing back inside as if a pack of dingoes was after her. I am sure she stood at the lounge room window for hours, trying to get up enough courage to go outside.

Early in the mornings she was also very active and this was her best chance to really get some speed up as she had the whole house as well as the yard to race through. In wet weather this could be a bit messy with not only muddy footprints but a long tail print as well!

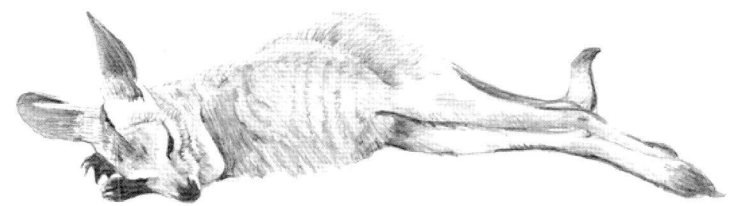

The dogs were shut outside and the door to the master bedroom was open and Lucky had a race track fit for the most active wallaroo. With the starting line in the far corner of her enclosure, she would build up speed as she crossed the yard and by the time she was in the door of the lounge room she was almost flying! The race track continued through the lounge room, across the family room, down the hall and ended at the finish line in our bedroom, in front of the mirrored doors of our wardrobe. Here Lucky would study the other wallaroo in the mirror while she got her breath back and then turn around and do the whole thing in reverse. For variety she had a slightly slower route which we named 'the mountain run.' This included jumping up and over the couch in the lounge room, over the dining room table in the family room and once in the bedroom, up and over our water bed. Don was usually still in bed reading the morning paper and would lift the paper out of the way as he heard her make the sharp turn from the hall into our bedroom, and call out;

'Here she comes again! Look out for the flying wallaroo!'

We had a brown woolly blanket which we kept on the end of the bed and on one occasion when she was doing her speed runs, this was left in a heap in the middle of the bedroom floor. Lucky's reaction to the blanket was astonishing! She leapt on the brown woolly 'animal', jumping up and down until it was well and truly flattened. She then stood back to study the results and happy it was not alive, picked up an armful of blanket and jumped around with it as though she had a dancing partner. Her behaviour was so enthusiastic that she eventually she fell over. What a sight that was! There was Lucky lying upside down with her fur on end and her legs and tail tangled in the blanket. Even now, Don and I still laugh over this.

We could never work out what caused this strange behaviour but it was so entertaining I often left the blanket on the floor so there would be repeat performances!

A game Lucky liked to include in her morning race track trials was 'the cat attack'. When Lucky first came to live with us she was smaller than the cat and definitely lower on the pecking order. Unfortunately for the cat this did not last long and within a few months Lucky towered over her and poor Bubby was back at the bottom of the ladder.

Lucky would be using the race track with great enthusiasm when she would suddenly make a detour to where Bubby was lying, stretched out asleep on the floor. She would stand quietly behind the cat and then quickly bend down and scoop Bubby up in her arms. Most of this very overweight black and white cat would be left dangling while Lucky grasped her in a strangle hold around the neck and shoulders. Bubby's eyes, which were normally big, would grow even bigger as she hung there waiting to be dropped back on the floor. When this finally happened, she would stagger away, fur standing on end, and collapse on the floor again. For some strange reason Bubby did not seem to be frightened of this rough handling and always made sure she was lying close to the 'race track' in the mornings. I think she was glad to have attention in a household that was more interested in dogs and wallaroos. Even when Lucky really got carried away and started jumping on Bubby after she was dropped on the floor to see if she made a noise, the cat still hung around for more!

Lucky progressed well after the setback of the thunder storm. As time went on she became a robust animal, full of health and vitality; sleepy by day and active by night. By the age of eighteen months she was eleven kilos in weight and in the wild would have been almost self reliant. She was still quite scared of the dark but in most other ways she was a confident teenager. Lucky had always been very much her 'own animal' and had kept her wild spirit in spite of living in luxury in our lounge room. Her place in the family circle was firmly established and we all knew what a gap she would leave once she was released. To stay with us indefinitely would have meant a life in captivity and we did not want this for her even if it had been possible.

My heart ached every time I thought about her release. It was like a dark cloud looming on my horizon. How I would miss her!

'Oh, Lucky, how will I ever give you up?' I would say sadly.

It was very important to find a release site before she got too big to handle and while she was young enough to adjust. The whole concept of a foster family was a short term thing and the aim was to return her to the wild well adjusted and healthy. I deliberately continued to give her a bottle night and morning though she did not really need it any more. This was the only way I could still get her into her pouch for easy handling but she really did look too big for it now.

I knew from a previous experience that she was already hard to handle. Not long before I had taken her to the local 'vet' to have her ears checked. Being inexperienced I had rejected the 'vet's' offer to give her a sedative before he looked at her. This was a *big* mistake and when he touched her she went wild. Though I was holding her tightly in

her pouch she kicked and bucked so much I was barely in control. Her back feet lashed out dangerously hitting me in the face, leaving angry red welts. 'Quick! Give her a Vitamin E shot or I'll end up with a broken nose!' I screamed holding on desperately.

Fortunately, the injection calmed her down immediately and the 'vet' was able to look at her ears and let us go home, pleased to get rid of us after our 'entertaining' visit. Lucky was exhausted and her hair was still standing out on end and I was shaking and covered in bruises when we finally got home.

'What on earth happened? You both look as though you have been pulled through the wringer backwards!' Don said, concerned for us but trying not to laugh. We must have looked a sorry sight!

This was a fortunate warning. Now I knew what could happen when I released her. I did not want to risk all the ground work I had put in. Some careful planning needed to be done. I wanted to find a place that would ease Lucky gently back into the wild and satisfy the wildlife organization that was in charge of her. When I made inquiries, the places suggested did not seem to have enough support for a joey who had no experience in the wild and did not even know what another wallaroo looked like. Happily, after asking some more questions, I found the perfect spot. When I drove out to look at the place my spirits rose the closer I came. A large mountain range stretched away into the distance and grassy foothills covered with rocky outcrops, sloped down into a long valley. What a place for a wallaroo! The property where Lucky would take her final steps towards the wild was owned by a couple who were dedicated to raising and releasing

wallabies and kangaroos. They had built a number of large paddocks where the animals could live safely while getting to know others of their own kind. Here they could become familiar with their surroundings before being released into the bush. I was to find out that this wonderful couple truly loved their charges and always put the interests of the animals before anything else. They invariably had a number of small joeys of varying ages in their care. These were kept in washing baskets in their kitchen and dining room, unless the joey was very small and then it would be kept under the covers of their double bed with the electric blanket turned on. Every so often there would be movement in one of the baskets and a face would appear or a joey would climb out and go for a tour of the kitchen before diving back into its basket. On the kitchen bench was a range of bottles and teats ready for the next round of feeds. Not only did they bottle feed the young ones in the house but also a number of older joeys in the paddocks who still needed special attention. It was funny to see them clustered round, all having their bottles at the same time. If they had a number of youngsters ready to go outside for exercise, the joeys were likely to be wheeled out to the paddock in a wheel barrow. To see them sitting together, enjoying the ride, was a sight to behold! Twice a day food was left out for the older animals who had 'gone bush'. They would straggle in, some with

their pouches bulging, others with joeys at heel and occasionally a male to 'supervise'.

Once I had made up my mind about Lucky the sense of loss caused me to shed some tears. but this was the only time I cried as I knew the story would have a happy ending.

I began to plan for her release day, knowing I needed to be well prepared. She definitely needed a sedative this time, as well as vitamin E and as I could not risk any trauma on the day, I arranged to have this given to her at home. Once she had drunk her early morning bottle I planned to sew her into the pouch this time so that there would be no wild leg flinging! 'Well Lucky, this is your big day! I hope you like your new home. It won't have the five star rating of your lounge room I'm afraid!' I said shakily.

I set off on the long journey full of apprehension. Lucky sat on the front seat with the belt firmly buckled, looking brightly over the top of her pouch. She did not seem to be at all drowsy, nor did she appear to be stressed as she studied the passing scenery. On the other hand I was shaking like a leaf and my stomach was tying itself in knots. I talked to her continually while I was driving and this settled us both down but it must have looked strange to passing drivers to see a woman having a lively conversation with what looked to be a large kangaroo in the front seat. Don followed behind just in case I broke down and to act as back up if a motorist took fright and called the police!

Lucky was still quite alert when we arrived and knew something different was in the air. She looked closely into my face as I carried her quietly into the paddock and then looked at her new surroundings as I knelt down with her in my arms.

'Here you are Lucky. Look! These animals are your own kind.'

All of a sudden she began to struggle and the last moments of her release were an undignified jumble as I tried to cut the ties holding her pouch. She eventually fell out of the pouch, landing in a heap with her lovely grey

and sandy-pink fur standing out on end. Once she had righted herself she stood clasping her arms across her chest taking in her surroundings. She did not look impressed with what she saw and if one of the wallabies came too close she thumped her back feet on the ground and looked very unfriendly. Lucky was going to take some time joining the mob!

A number of female wallabies and wallaroos already lived in Lucky's paddock and she did not like the look of any of them. The wallaroos, called Sabrina and Gabriella were very interested in Lucky and tried to get a closer look but she was not having any of this and took off, thumping her feet on the ground loudly to emphasize her feelings. She avoided them by making for a rocky area shaded by trees, where she could keep her distance and hide amongst the rocks.

I spent the rest of the day with her and she stayed close to me unless another animal came near. When I offered her the pouch she was very happy to tumble in and study the paddock safely from here, too tired to pretend she was a brave wallaroo any longer. I gave her a bottle and reassured her until it got dark. The night was going to be a big test for her. I could not sit out with her all night, though I had arranged to stay on the farm for the next few days to see her through the worst of it. Poor Lucky, alone in a paddock with a mob of strange animals and afraid of the dark as well!

Next morning her expression said it all. '*Can I go back to my lounge room now please?*' She had managed to survive the night and was very glad to see me but she looked very weary. Her feet were bruised and cut from jumping on the rocks to keep away from her 'friends'. The soft life at

home had not prepared her for this. She dived into her pouch when I offered it and fell asleep on my lap exhausted from being constantly on the move all night. It was going to be a hard time for Lucky!

The days were not so bad as she could doze in the sun while keeping half an eye on me, but the nights must have been frightening and to make matters worse it rained heavily all one night and she was drenched to the skin. In spite of all this she survived, her feisty nature giving her the stamina, and I finally left her, knowing she would be in caring hands. In the first few weeks I made the long trip to see Lucky twice a week and enjoyed being with her and watching life on the 'kangaroo farm'. Eventually my visits became less frequent until I only visited every few months. Lucky always knew me when I came and would look up when I called, recognizing the sound of my voice. At this stage she was very independent and had adjusted well to her life on the farm. By then I was the only one she allowed close to her and we would sit together in the paddock while I chatted to her and stroked her fur. She enjoyed the presents I brought her; the long soft grass from our home paddock, the pecan nuts and of course the tea in her tea bowl!

'When do you think you will become a wild wallaroo, Lucky?' I would ask when I saw her gazing longingly at the hills beyond the fence.

Lucky gave me her answer a few months later. She did not make friends with the other animals in her paddock but stayed a loner, true to her kind. One day she must have made up her mind in was time to go and escaped, leaving her old world behind. She came back occasionally to feed and then disappeared altogether. Lucky was a wild wallaroo again.

I had kept my part of the bargain, to raise her and let her go free.

PART THREE

RETURN TO THE WILD

High on a rocky outcrop an adult wallaroo looked down into the valley below. She had been browsing most of the night and was preparing for sleep on her favourite rock ledge, safe from any danger. She knew the best places to eat, down on the slopes, where water seeped down the rock faces and kept the grass long and soft well into the dry season. She also knew the best tracks to follow between the rocks and through the tall timber, which she could follow without being noticed. Being a wallaroo meant she was a shy and solitary animal who liked to watch life in the bush around her without being seen and melt back into the shadows if anything came too close.

As she crouched there, familiar sounds drifted up to her as life in the valley began to stir. A small flock of galahs called to each other in their tree, a rooster crowed, a man spoke cheerfully to his animals and a dog barked an answer. The wallaroo knew these sounds well as they came from a farm yard at the bottom of the valley where she had spent many months in a large enclosed paddock. She still remembered snatches of her time there, particularly the wheat and corn she liked to eat and the other animals who seemed to enjoy being to-gether. She remembered longing to escape from the paddock so she could be free and on her own and how she patrolled the fences every night looking for a way to get out.

Eventually she had found a hole big enough to clamber through and had finally gone free.

The memory of the food had lured her back once or twice when she was tired and hungry but she had become restless once inside the paddock. When she found the hole was blocked up she had bounded towards the fence and cleared it in a leap. She would not go back again.

Months later she had developed into a strong, hardy animal, who was sure of herself in the bush and could look after herself in any conditions. She could bound across the rocks and up the gullies with sure footed speed and she knew the special places to go if a man or a dingo invaded her territory. Even in the driest times she could find enough to eat and when the water spots dried up she found she could still survive. The unpredictable quality of her life was stimulating after her time at the farm and she was prepared to endure some hardships to have her freedom.

Now she felt a extra sense of satisfaction as a new life stirred, a tiny joey had already attached itself to a teat in her pouch after making the journey safely through the fur. She felt contentment, as though her life was now complete and what she was designed to do was at last fulfilled. This made up for the rude intrusion when a large male wallaroo had chased her through the bush and mated with her. She had felt uneasy at this invasion of her private world but when the other wallaroo did not come back she settled down again to her peaceful ways.

As she lay dozing on the ledge, snatches of a more distant life came back, when she had been a small joey, afraid, without her mother. She remembered the woman who had rescued and raised her, remembered feeling safe and warm and playing sparring games with the woman who had no fur. In a language the wallaroo did not understand, the woman had talked to her and one word stayed to echo in her mind..........

'Lucky'

Lyn Ellison was inspired by the magical friendship with a white-backed magpie to change direction in her career from potter and sculptor to become a painter of Australian wildlife. Magpies are still her favourite subject but she has become passionate about all wild birds and animals. From her home in the Coomera Valley in Queensland she has a wealth subjects to base her paintings on; the ones she sees every day living their lives with patience and fortitude. She also likes to explore the Australian bush looking for inspiration. It was on one of these trips that she found Lucky the wallaroo. The following twelve months was such a joy she felt she had to share the experience. The story and the illustrations were a labour of love and she hopes the reader will enjoy this touching story.   .

Lyn's original paintings are found in a number of galleries in Australia, including 'Gull Cottage' and 'Mitchell's Gallery' in Queensland, 'Treetops Griffith Gallery' in New South Wales and 'Wise Possum Gallery' in Victoria. She has produced 7 limited edition prints, mostly published by Origin Publishing, many of which are sold out. Lyn has won a number of wildlife painting prizes and had a successful solo exhibition. It was at a joint exhibition with fellow artist Peta Boyce that the idea to write and illustrate books about the wonderful characters that have come into their care, evolved. 'Wild About You - Friends With Feathers' is the second book in the series with the majority of the bird stories by Peta Boyce.   .

Acknowledgements; On behalf of Lucky, Lyn would like to thank the following people for their good advice and care. Glenda Davis, Orm and Nancy Ridgway, Jan Iredell and Michael Woodcock of Michael Higgins Veterinary Surgery. Lyn would also like to thank these people for their help in making this book possible. Don Ellison for his publishing experience, Anthony Ellison, Kelly and Merryon Ryall for their computer skills, Noel and Margaret Hewitt for their proof reading, Kay Collett of Applause Press for printing advice and Jeff and Pauline Durston of 'Gull Cottage' for their interest in Lyn's art work. A special thanks to Peta Boyce, co-author of the book 'Friends With Feathers' who shared moments of panic and also the red wine. To the family members Don and Merryon, thanks for putting up with a wallaroo in the lounge room and helping to raise Lucky.   .